Construction

JOY GREGORY

LIGHTBOX
openlightbox.com

Lightbox is an all-inclusive digital solution for the teaching and learning of curriculum topics in an original, groundbreaking way. Lightbox is based on National Curriculum Standards.

STANDARD FEATURES OF LIGHTBOX

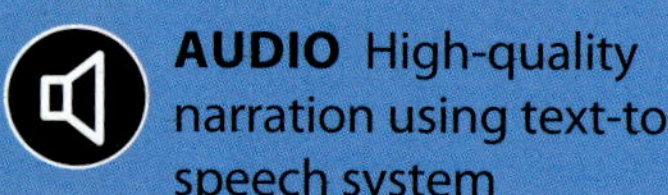
AUDIO High-quality narration using text-to-speech system

ACTIVITIES Printable PDFs that can be emailed and graded

SLIDESHOWS Pictorial overviews of key concepts

VIDEOS Embedded high-definition video clips

WEBLINKS Curated links to external, child-safe resources

TRANSPARENCIES Step-by-step layering of maps, diagrams, charts, and timelines

INTERACTIVE MAPS Interactive maps and aerial satellite imagery

QUIZZES Ten multiple choice questions that are automatically graded and emailed for teacher assessment

KEY WORDS Matching key concepts to their definitions

CONTENTS

Construction in the United States

Most buildings in the United States were built by the construction industry. That includes homes and apartment buildings, urban skyscrapers, shopping malls, barns, and backyard decks. The sector also builds institutional properties, such as hospitals and schools.

There are **730,000 construction companies** in the United States.

The U.S. construction industry generates **$1.7 trillion every year.**

It takes **13,127 feet** (4 kilometers) of **lumber** to frame the **average** single-family home in the United States.

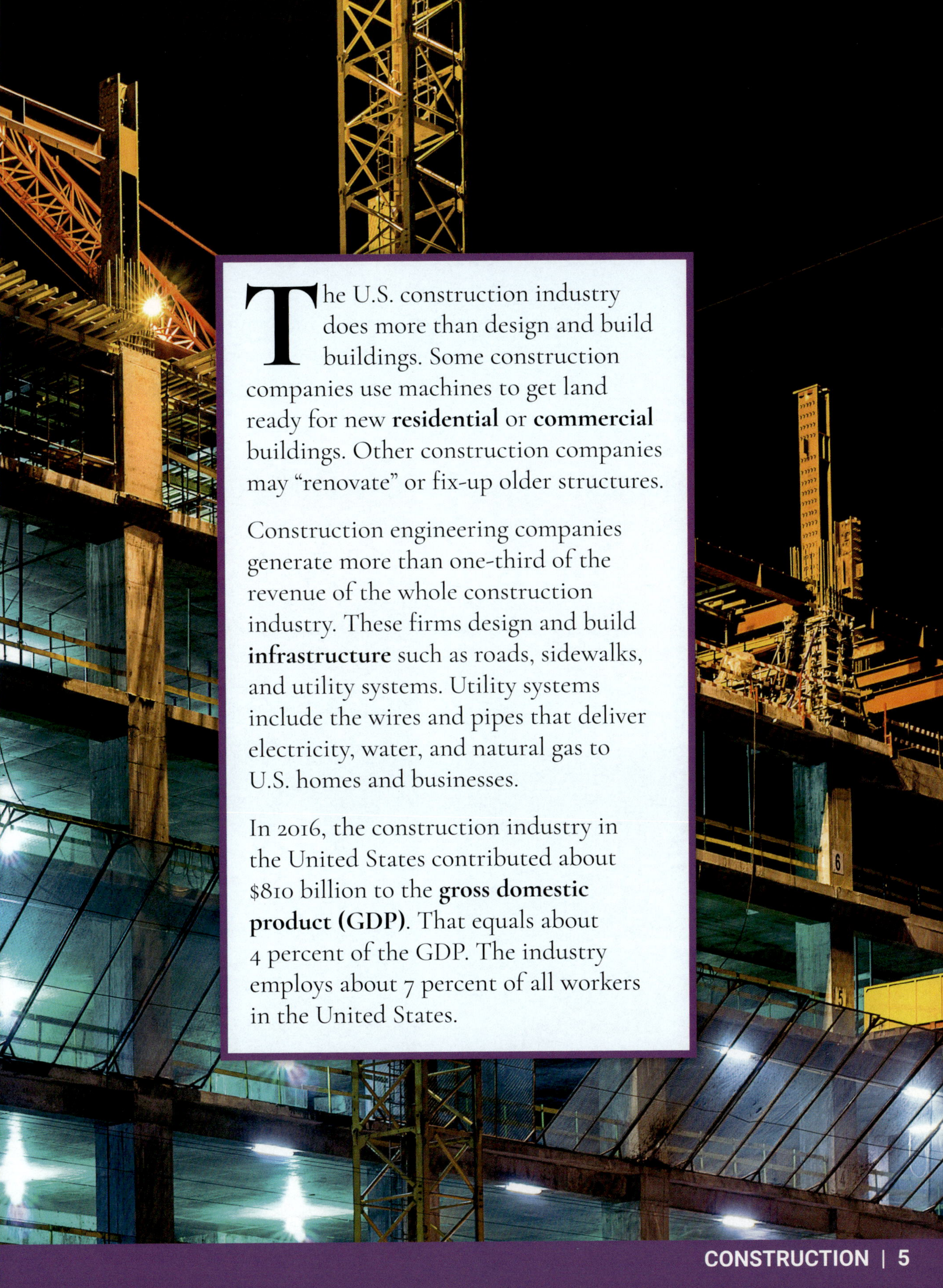

The U.S. construction industry does more than design and build buildings. Some construction companies use machines to get land ready for new **residential** or **commercial** buildings. Other construction companies may "renovate" or fix-up older structures.

Construction engineering companies generate more than one-third of the revenue of the whole construction industry. These firms design and build **infrastructure** such as roads, sidewalks, and utility systems. Utility systems include the wires and pipes that deliver electricity, water, and natural gas to U.S. homes and businesses.

In 2016, the construction industry in the United States contributed about $810 billion to the **gross domestic product (GDP)**. That equals about 4 percent of the GDP. The industry employs about 7 percent of all workers in the United States.

Construction Then and Now

The first builders in the United States were **indigenous** people. Over time, European settlers arrived. As more people moved into towns and cities for work, the construction industry changed to meet the needs of a more **industrialized** society.

Building Homes

Some indigenous peoples built wooden longhouses that housed several families. Today, most U.S. homes contain one family. Modern builders use a variety of materials, such as wood and cement.

THEN

NOW

Developing Communities

Some Native American peoples moved their communities from place to place, depending on the season. Today, people live in one place. U.S. homes are built around roads and utility systems.

THEN

NOW

The modern construction industry depends on workers who have special training and skills. Some work with plumbing or electrical wiring. Others frame houses or pour concrete. Construction engineering is also specialized. Some construction engineers build roads. Others build utility systems.

Modern machines and computers have changed the construction industry. These **innovations** cut the cost of construction. They also reduced the time construction takes. Over the last century, the construction industry developed more health and safety rules. Some workers may now have to wear safety helmets, glasses, vests, and boots.

Barn Raising

Pioneers worked together to build barns. Most of today's barns are built by paid construction workers. Many barns include walls and doors that are built in factories and shipped to the construction site.

Building Infrastructure

Western towns often had a Main Street where people bought supplies. Today's infrastructure includes more than streets. Communities are connected by plumbing, electricity, internet cables, parks, and bike paths.

Construction across the United States

The U.S. construction industry operates from coast to coast. The sector provides homes and workplaces for a population of more than 326 million people. Much construction is concentrated in the country's largest cities, and in large, growing metropolitan areas in states such as Washington, Oregon, and Florida.

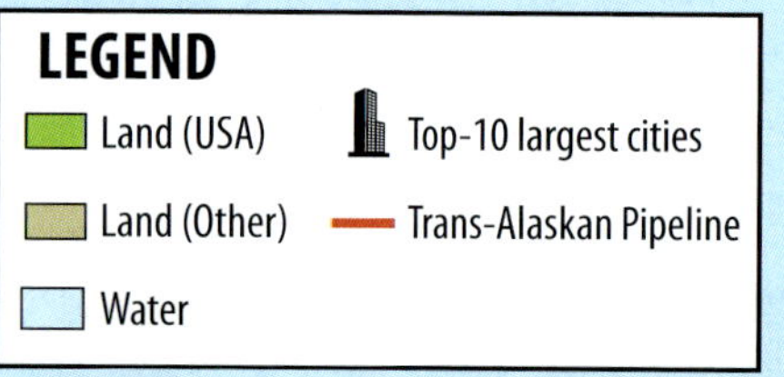

SCALE

400 MILES

700 KILOMETERS

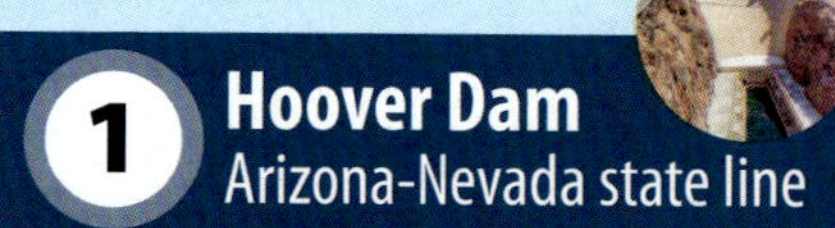

1 Hoover Dam
Arizona-Nevada state line

Hoover Dam was the first mega U.S. construction project. Built in the 1930s, it generated electricity for Arizona, Nevada, and part of California. The dam rises 726 feet (221 m) above Black Canyon.

2 Trans-Alaskan Pipeline
Alaska

The Trans-Alaska Pipeline moves oil 800 miles (1,300 km) from Prudhoe Bay to Valdez on the Gulf of Alaska. About half the pipeline is above ground. This allows wild animals to walk underneath.

3 One World Trade Center New York

One World Trade Center is the tallest building in the United States. Finished in 2014, it is 1,776 feet (541 m) high. That includes the observation deck and antenna. The tower has 104 stories. It is the sixth-tallest building in the world.

4 Reconstruction Texas, Florida, Puerto Rico

After disasters like the hurricanes that hit Texas, Florida, and Puerto Rico in 2017, reconstruction boosts demand for building supplies and workers. The construction industry restores infrastructure for power, transportation, and communications.

Construction and the U.S. Economy

A healthy economy is good news for the construction industry. When people have jobs and are making money, they hire construction companies to build new homes or restore old houses. If the economy is strong, companies also hire constructors to improve their offices and factories.

Electricians are the largest group of skilled tradespeople working in the United States. The next-largest category includes plumbers, pipefitters, and steamfitters.

In a strong economy, people and businesses also pay more taxes. Governments use tax money for buildings and infrastructure. **Federal**, state, and local governments spend more than $416 billion a year on infrastructure. U.S. companies that build buildings make about $748 billion a year. Engineering construction firms make about $260 billion a year on design and engineering projects.

Governments invest about **$165 billion** a year on **U.S. highways**.

The average **construction company** employee earns **$45,200** a year.

Many big construction firms have construction and engineering units. The country's largest construction companies are "general contractors." These firms hire skilled and unskilled workers to design and build construction projects. Two-thirds of all of the construction firms in the U.S. are "specialty trade contractors." These companies complete specific parts of construction jobs, such as digging basements, making cabinets, or laying pipes.

Timeline of Construction Events

Construction has always been a hands-on business. Many jobs require little training. The demand for skilled workers grows as new materials, equipment, and design are used.

1750	1800	1850	1875	1900

1775. The Wilderness Road connects Virginia and Kentucky. The road is built with axes, saws, and shovels.

1869. The Trans-Continental Railroad opens, linking Iowa to the Pacific Coast. This is the first railroad to cross a continent.

1885. The Home Insurance Building in Chicago opens. The world's first skyscraper has 10 stories.

1933. The Tennessee Valley Authority System construction starts. The series of hydroelectric dams and power plants provides cheap electricity to homes and businesses and helps prevent floods.

Future. Housing will dominate the future of the U.S. construction industry. As the country's population grows, people will seek safe, affordable housing.

1920 | 1940 | 1950 | 2000 | THE FUTURE

1947. Levittown construction begins on Long Island, New York. The housing development is the model for **suburbs** that are being built across the nation.

1956. President Dwight D. Eisenhower authorizes construction of the Interstate Highway System.

U.S. Construction in the World

The United States has the world's second-largest construction industry. Only China has a bigger construction industry. Several of the largest construction and engineering firms in the United States also do business in other countries.

The United States will export $857 million of windows and doors in 2018. That equals seven percent of global demand for windows and doors.

Many countries also **import** construction products made in the United States. Nearly 60 percent of U.S. construction exports go to just four countries. Canada, Mexico, China, and Japan are the biggest importers of U.S. construction products.

Around the world, construction industry customers want buildings and infrastructure that use modern technology. U.S. companies lead the way in innovation. Some of the new technology saves people money because it is more efficient. For example, home owners, businesses, and **municipal** governments want energy-efficient lighting for their homes, companies, and streets.

U.S. exports of **wood products** were expected to hit **$18 billion** in **2018**.

Mexico imports **80 percent** of its air conditioning systems from the **UNITED STATES**.

Exports of construction materials and technology are important to the U.S. construction industry's growth. Key exports from the United States include heating, ventilation, air conditioning, and refrigeration products and equipment. The country also exports lighting, plumbing equipment such as pipes and pumps, wood products, insulation materials, windows, and doors. Exports of these products are expected to increase to $40 billion in 2018.

The United States imports more construction products than it exports. It is the world's largest importer of construction products. The United States imports more than $60 billion of building products every year. Much of the lumber used to build U.S.-made houses comes from trees grown in Canada. Other major sources of imported lumber are Germany, Sweden, and Russia. China is a major source of flooring material and steel imports to the United States.

Wood is imported to the United States as logs, which are then sent to U.S. factories to be turned into boards and other wood products.

Facing the Issues

Millions of Americans depend on construction industry jobs for money to house and feed their families. With more Americans needing homes and more infrastructure in need of repair and upgrades, the industry's economic value will rise in the future. This good news, however, is lessened by the industry's environmental impact.

Some construction industry products increase greenhouse gas **emissions** linked to climate change. The industry's switch to using more energy-efficient products, including solar power, better insulation, and energy-saving windows, will help. New buildings and infrastructure products also improve water conservation. Examples include low-water toilets and low-flow showerheads or kitchen taps.

Rainwater management systems reduce flooding and allow homeowners and businesses to use rainwater, instead of tap water, to irrigate outdoor landscapes.

Debate

One-third of all the energy used in the world runs buildings. Most of this energy comes from **nonrenewable** sources. Net-zero-energy buildings (NZEB) use renewable sources to generate about the same amount of energy that they use. Should governments **legislate** NZEB?

YES

- NZEB structures cut greenhouse gases by reducing the amount of nonrenewable energy needed to power, heat, or cool homes.
- NZEB technology cuts homeowners' energy bills.
- Laws that increase demand for NZEB materials will open export markets for U.S. companies.

NO

- NZEB currently requires solar panels, which work poorly on office towers or apartment buildings.
- It is expensive to add NZEB technology to existing buildings.
- A focus on NZEB might ignore other environmental issues related to water conservation and transportation.

Solar panels on the roofs of new homes not only help to decrease heating bills but also help to protect the environment.

Looking to the Future

In the United States and around the world, the construction industry plays an important role in people's lives. The buildings where people live, work, and play are impacted by discussions about climate change and human safety. Severe weather systems, including tornadoes, hurricanes, and floods, boost the demand to build structures and infrastructure that can stand up to extreme weather.

As more people move into urban areas, governments also face issues about "densification," or how many people can and should live in a particular area. Sustainability is another concern. Scientists advise governments about how buildings and infrastructure affect wildlife and human habitats, including air quality, access to light and air, and access to green spaces.

Labor shortages are another possible concern for the construction industry. Some industry insiders say the U.S. construction industry is already short 20 percent of the workers it needs. Experts predict that demand for construction labor will be higher than in any other sector in the country over the next decade. To encourage young Americans to choose construction industry jobs, some companies offer free training programs and increased employee benefits.

One way construction companies are trying to prevent a shortage of labor is by training young people in skilled trade such as bricklaying, plumbing, and electrical engineering.

Careers in Construction

A career in construction is a good choice for people who like to work with their hands. Construction work takes place in a variety of indoor and outdoor environments. Most jobs involve teamwork and problem solving. Many construction sites include jobs for nonskilled labor. About 10 percent of U.S. construction workers are female.

Skilled Tradesperson
Skilled tradespeople handle specific tasks on construction sites. They include pipe fitters, carpenters, iron workers, crane operators, and people who work with heating, ventilation, and air conditioning (HVAC) systems.

Duties: Carries out specific tasks on construction sites.

Education: **Apprenticeship** training

Interests: Construction, problem solving, hands-on work

Cost Estimator
Cost estimators provide information about how much a construction job will cost. Estimators collect construction and engineering data for specific jobs. They use the data to calculate how much time, money, materials, and labor are needed to build a building or infrastructure project.

Duties: Predicts the costs and timelines of construction projects

Education: Bachelor's degree in physical sciences, math, engineering or statistics

Interests: Construction details, record keeping, math

Structural Engineer
Structural engineers design structures such as buildings, bridges, and tunnels. Many work with architects or contractors who design buildings or infrastructure projects. Their expertise helps workers build structures that stand up to natural and human-made forces.

Duties: Provides advice about materials and construction methods

Education: Bachelor's degree in engineering

Interests: Construction, attention to detail, problem solving

Activity

Bridge Building Research Project

The longest over-water bridge in the world stretches 24 miles (39 km) over Lake Pontchartrain in Louisiana. From 1929 to 2003, the 1,053-foot-high (0.3 km) Royal Gorge Bridge in Colorado was the highest bridge in the world. That record was broken in 2003, when a higher bridge opened in China.

Construction engineers design bridges for different situations. Some bridges move motor vehicles and trains above or under highways. Other bridges move traffic between islands or across water-soaked land, such as marshes or swamps, where it is difficult to build a road.

Research bridges in the United States. You will need:

- Notebook or paper
- Pen or pencil to record findings
- Colored pencils or paints
- Access to your school library or the internet

Instructions

1. Use your school library or the internet to research bridges in the United States. Find two examples of bridges.
2. For each bridge, find three items that make that bridge interesting. Is the bridge supported by cables, support columns, or beams? Is it made of steel, concrete, or wood? How high or long is the bridge? Is the bridge used by pedestrians, automobiles, or trains?
3. Use colored pencils or paints to illustrate one of the three most-interesting facts about each bridge. For example: Draw the pillars that support the bridge, or the draw the bridge and note its length or height.

Quiz

Check out how much you have learned about construction in the United States. The answers to all these questions are in this book.

ONE
What is the name of the community that became a model for suburban communities across the United States?

TWO
How many feet of lumber does it take to frame the average single-family home in the United States?

THREE
What is the tallest building in the United States?

FOUR
What country imports more construction products than any other in the world?

FIVE
What was the first mega-construction project in the United States?

SIX
How many construction companies does the U.S. have?

SEVEN
What percent does the construction industry contribute to the GDP?

EIGHT
What country imports the most U.S. construction products?

TEN
Carpenters, plumbers, and crane operators are examples of what type of job?

NINE
What percentage of U.S. workers are employed by the construction industry?

ANSWERS
ONE Levittown **TWO** 13,127 feet (4 km) **THREE** One World Trade Center **FOUR** The United States **FIVE** Hoover Dam **SIX** 730,000 **SEVEN** 4 percent **EIGHT** Canada **NINE** 7 percent **TEN** Skilled tradespeople

Key Words

apprenticeship: a period of on-the-job training

commercial: a for-profit business

emissions: waste products that are released as gases

exports: the act of selling a product to another country

federal: the central government, not state

gross domestic product (GDP): the dollar value of all goods and services produced in a given time and place

import: to buy goods from other countries

indigenous: something that lives or grows naturally in a region; not brought in

industrialized: factory-based

infrastructure: the services needed to run a community, state or country, includes roads, utilities, hospitals, and schools

innovations: new ideas, objects or ways or doing things

institutional: relating to a hospital, school, or government office

legislate: to make laws about

municipal: the government of a city or town

nonrenewable: describes a source of energy that will eventually run out

pioneers: the first people to do something new

residential: having to do with housing

suburbs: neighborhoods outside of the central business district

urban: relating to a city

Index

LIGHTBOX

SUPPLEMENTARY RESOURCES

Click on the plus icon ⊕ found in the bottom left corner of each spread to open additional teacher resources.

- Download and print the book's quizzes and activities
- Access curriculum correlations
- Explore additional web applications that enhance the Lightbox experience

LIGHTBOX DIGITAL TITLES
Packed full of integrated media

VIDEOS

INTERACTIVE MAPS

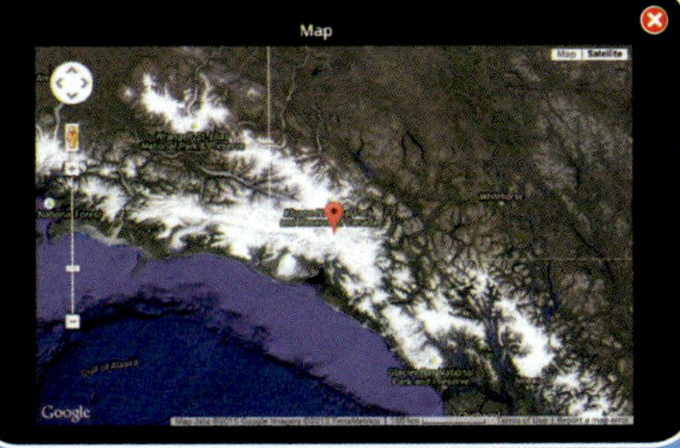

WEBLINKS

SLIDESHOWS

QUIZZES

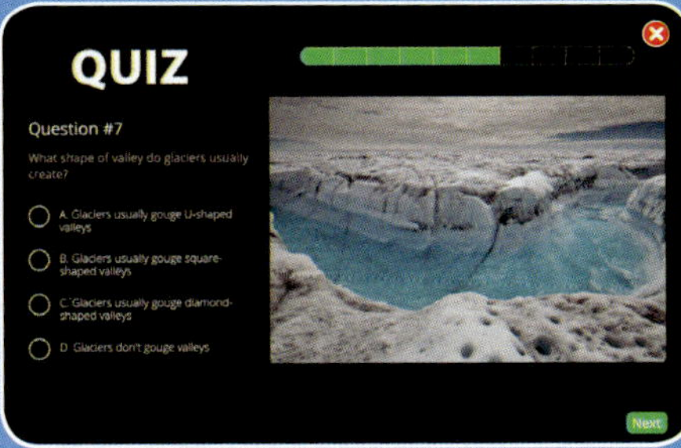

OPTIMIZED FOR

- ✓ TABLETS
- ✓ WHITEBOARDS
- ✓ COMPUTERS
- ✓ AND MUCH MORE!

Published by Smartbook Media Inc.
350 5th Avenue, 59th Floor New York, NY 10118
Website: www.openlightbox.com

Project Coordinator: Heather Kissock
Art Director: Terry Paulhus

Library of Congress Cataloging-in-Publication Data
Names: Gregory, Joy, author.
Title: Construction / Joy Gregory.
Description: New York, NY : Smartbook Media Inc., [2019] | Series: American industries | Includes index.
Identifiers: LCCN 2017055661 (print) | LCCN 2017058126 (ebook) | ISBN 9781510535633 (Multi User ebook) | ISBN 9781510535626 (hardcover : alk. paper)
Subjects: LCSH: Construction industry--United States--History--Juvenile literature.
Classification: LCC HD9715.U52 (ebook) | LCC HD9715.U52 G726 2019 (print) |
DDC 338.4/76240973--dc23
LC record available at https://lccn.loc.gov/2017055661

Printed in Brainerd, Minnesota, United States
1 2 3 4 5 6 7 8 9 0 22 21 20 19 18

042018
120517

Every reasonable effort has been made to trace ownership and to obtain permission to reprint copyright material. The publisher would be pleased to have any errors or omissions brought to its attention so that they may be corrected in subsequent printings.
The publisher acknowledges Getty Images, Alamy, Newscom, Shutterstock, and iStock as its primary image suppliers for this title.